THE MAGNIFICENT BOOK OF DINOSAURS

AND OTHER PREHISTORIC CREATURES

THE MAGNIFICENT BOOK OF DINOSAURS

AND OTHER PREHISTORIC CREATURES

Illustrated by
Rudolf Farkas

Written by
Tom Jackson

weldonowen

weldon**owen**

Published by Weldon Owen Children's Books
An imprint of Weldon Owen International, L.P.
A subsidiary of Insight Editions
PO Box 3088
San Rafael, CA 94912
www.insighteditions.com

INSIGHT EDITIONS
CEO: Raoul Goff
Art Director: Stuart Smith
Production Manager: Deena Hashem

WELDON OWEN CHILDREN'S BOOKS
Designer: Rod Teasdale
Senior Editor: Lydia Halliday
Assistant Editor: Pandita Geary

Written by Tom Jackson
Illustrated by Rudolf Farkas
Additional Illustrations by Simon Mendez
Consultant: Dr. Dave Martill, University of Portsmouth

ISBN: 979-8-88674-433-0

Manufactured in China
First printing, April 2023 RRD0093609

10 9 8 7 6 5 4 3 2 1

REPLANTED PAPER

Insight Editions, in association with Roots of Peace, will plant two trees for each tree used in the manufacturing of this book.

FSC www.fsc.org MIX Paper | Supporting responsible forestry FSC® C144853

Introduction

Millions of years ago, during the Mesozoic Era, prehistoric reptiles called dinosaurs roamed the Earth. It was a very different Earth then. The continents were connected, the land that people live on today was covered in water, and lush forests provided the perfect environment for dinosaurs to thrive. But about 65 million years ago, a large asteroid struck Earth and caused the dinosaurs to become extinct. So everything we know about them comes from the bits and pieces of their bodies that became fossils.

This book features stunning illustrations of the mysterious dinosaurs that once lived on Earth—from gigantic plant-eaters to swift and deadly predators. Each page showcases a different creature, such as *Tyrannosaurus rex* or *Stegosaurus*, with fascinating facts that illustrate how the dinosaurs lived.

Which dinosaur had thick thumb spikes? Which one had a tail like a club that it used to whack enemies? Which dinosaur was twice as tall as a giraffe? Discover all of these answers and more as you enter *The Magnificent Book of Dinosaurs and Other Prehistoric Creatures.*

Fact file

Found in: North Africa
Meaning of name: Spine lizard
Length: 59 ft (18 m)
Weight: 8,800 lb (4,000 kg)
Lived: 95–70 million years ago
Diet: Fish

Contents

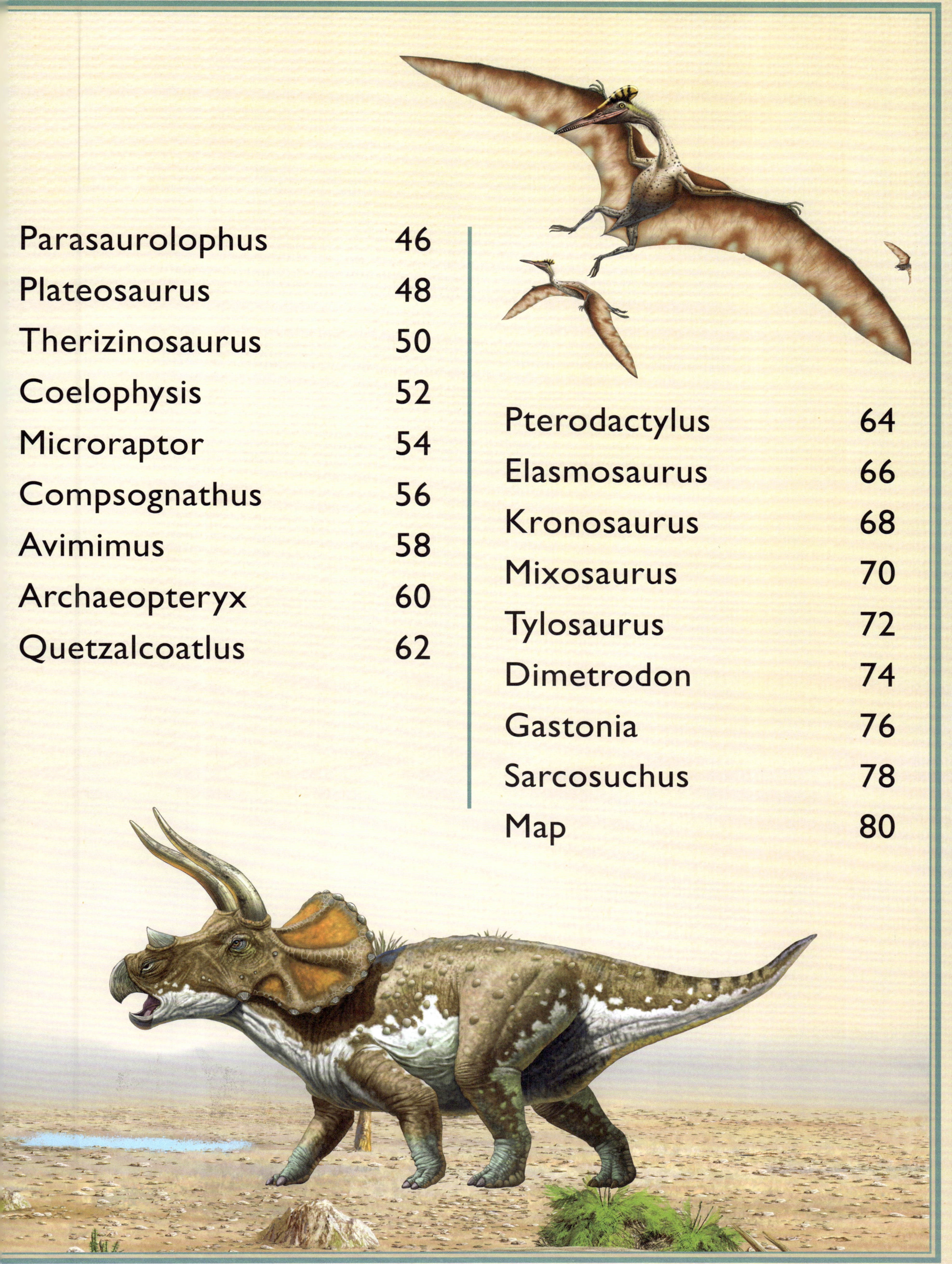

Tyrannosaurus rex

- *T. rex*'s curved teeth were serrated like a shark's.
- Research suggests that *T. rex* could swallow up to 500 pounds (230 kg) of meat in one gulp.
- This dinosaur's small arms had long, hooked claws for ripping up meat and for hanging on to its prey.

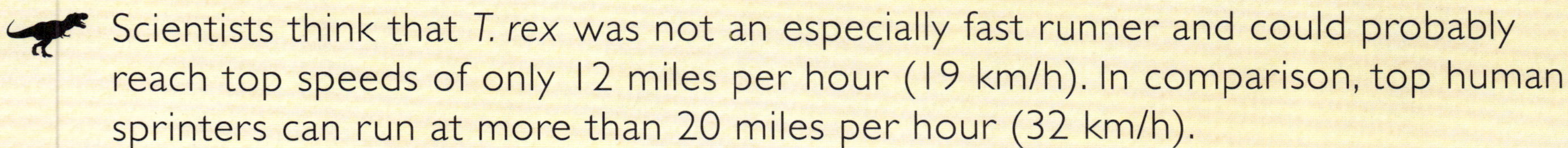

- Scientists think that *T. rex* was not an especially fast runner and could probably reach top speeds of only 12 miles per hour (19 km/h). In comparison, top human sprinters can run at more than 20 miles per hour (32 km/h).
- The bones of some *T. rex* fossils have *T. rex* tooth marks in them. This suggests they fought each other.
- *T. rex* had the strongest bite of any land animal that ever lived.
- In addition to hunting for food, *T. rex* also ate the remains of dead dinosaurs.

Fact file

Found in: North America

Meaning of name: King of the tyrant lizards

Length: Up to 42 ft (13 m)

Weight: Up to 19,555 lb (8,870 kg)

Lived: 68–66 million years ago

Diet: Other dinosaurs

Giganotosaurus

- This giant hunter was even larger than *T. rex*, but it was more slender and a faster runner.
- *Giganotosaurus* may have teamed up into hunting packs to attack herds of plant-eating dinosaurs.
- Its long, thin tail helped the massive animal stay balanced as it ran.
- *Giganotosaurus*'s head was more than five feet (1.5 m) long!

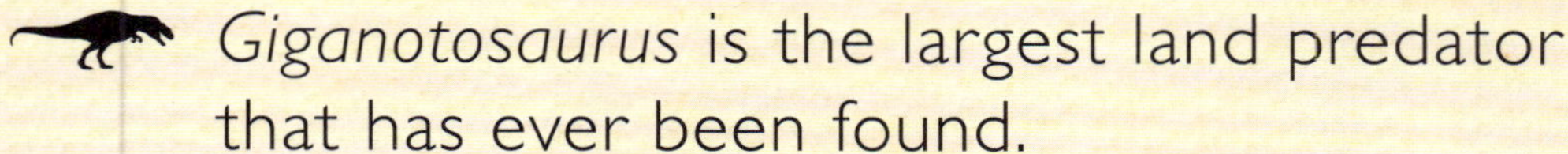

- *Giganotosaurus* is the largest land predator that has ever been found.
- Each of its teeth had sawlike edges, which allowed it to cut through flesh easily.

Fact file

Found in: Argentina

Meaning of name: Giant southern lizard

Length: 41 ft (12.5 m)

Weight: 17,600 lb (7,980 kg)

Lived: 112–90 million years ago

Diet: Other dinosaurs

Allosaurus

- *Allosaurus* had hooked teeth, which would have helped it to hold on to its struggling prey.
- *Allosaurus* sometimes lost teeth during fights, but they grew back throughout its life.
- This hunter may have killed its prey by biting their necks.
- *Allosaurus* was one of the most common predators in North America during the late Jurassic Period.
- The dinosaur had tough ridges on its forehead, which protected its eyes during fights.

 A powerful sense of smell helped *Allosaurus* to find prey.

 This dinosaur is known to have preyed on stegosaurs.

Fact file

Found in: North America, Europe
Meaning of name: Different lizard
Length: 39 ft (12 m)
Weight: 4,400 lb (2,000 kg)
Lived: 156–150 million years ago
Diet: Other dinosaurs

Deinonychus

Fact file

Found in: North America

Meaning of name: Terrible claw

Length: 10 ft (3 m)

Weight: 165 lb (75 kg)

Lived: 120–110 million years ago

Diet: Meat

- This fast-running dinosaur could kill its prey by slashing them with the long, curved claw on each hind limb.
- The large killer claws were retractable, so they did not scrape along the ground—this kept the claws sharp.
- Scientists think *Deinonychus* may have used its hooked claws to climb trees to escape from larger hunters.
- *Deinonychus* was probably covered in feathers that were very similar to those of today's birds, but they did not help it to fly.
- *Deinonychus* ran on two legs. Its front legs were used for grabbing prey.
- *Deinonychus* had a relatively large brain for its body size, so it was probably one of the smarter dinosaurs.

Utahraptor

- The long bones of a *Utahraptor* were hollow but strong. The bones did not weigh very much, which may have helped *Utahraptor* move quickly.
- *Utahraptor*'s mighty claws could have been used for stabbing or slashing its prey.
- A coat of feathers probably kept it warm and helped it to attract mates.

- *Utahraptor* may have flapped its arms like wings in order to help it climb steep slopes.
- *Utahraptor* probably had good eyesight, so it could spot prey from far away.
- Scientists think that *Utahraptor* could jump 15 feet (4.5 m) in one leap.
- Evidence suggests that *Utahraptor* may have hunted in packs to kill larger animals.

Fact file

Found in: North America

Meaning of name: Utah's predator

Length: 20 ft (6 m)

Weight: 2,200 lb (1,000 kg)

Lived: 112–100 million years ago

Diet: Other dinosaurs

Spinosaurus

- This is the largest carnivorous dinosaur ever to be discovered.
- *Spinosaurus* hunted in water and may have grabbed animals from riverbanks, like crocodiles do today.
- This dinosaur is named for the long spines that stick out of its back.
- *Spinosaurus* could stand on its back legs and grab animals with its long arms.
- Its bony spines were covered with a "sail" of skin that might have helped it regulate its body temperature or attract mates.

- *Spinosaurus* had nostrils on the top of its snout so it could hide below the water with just the top of its head showing.
- This hunter had sensors on its snout that helped it detect water currents and the weak electrical signals made by large fish swimming nearby.

Fact file

Found in: North Africa

Meaning of name: Spine lizard

Length: 59 ft (18 m)

Weight: 8,800 lb (4,000 kg)

Lived: 95–70 million years ago

Diet: Fish

Iguanodon

- This dinosaur's fossils were discovered in 1820. It was the second type of dinosaur to be identified by scientists.
- *Iguanodon* had a thick spiked claw on each thumb.
- Early scientists mistakenly thought *Iguanodon's* thumb spike was a nose horn.
- *Iguanodon* was probably able to move around on two or four legs.

Fact file

Found in: Europe
Meaning of name: Iguana tooth
Length: 33 ft (10 m)
Weight: 8,800 lb (4,000 kg)
Lived: 140–110 million years ago
Diet: Plants

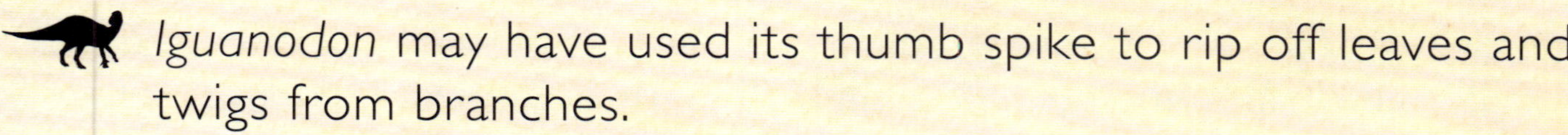

- *Iguanodon* may have used its thumb spike to rip off leaves and twigs from branches.
- Evidence suggests that these plant-eaters lived in large herds.
- *Iguanodon* could use its clawed thumb to defend itself from other dinosaurs.

Triceratops

- *Triceratops* used its long horns to fight off attacks by large meat-eaters like *T. rex*.
- The back of *Triceratops*'s head was covered with a large bony frill that protected its neck from predators.
- *Triceratops* had the biggest skull of any land animal that has ever lived. One fossilized skull measured more than eight feet (2.5 m) long.

Fact file

Found in: North America

Meaning of name: Three-horned face

Length: 30 ft (9 m)

Weight: 12,000 lb (5,440 kg)

Lived: 68–66 million years ago

Diet: Plants

- The horns above its eyes were more than three feet (1 m) long.
- *Triceratops* had a hooked beak that could cut up leaves and small branches.
- *Triceratops* was not a fast runner, but it likely charged its enemies to chase them away.

Stygimoloch

- This dinosaur is a young *Pachycephalosaurus*. In the past, it was thought that the *Stygimoloch* was a different type of dinosaur altogether.
- This dinosaur had a domed skull covered in sharp, pointed horns.
- Scientists believe that the creature's spiked head was used mostly for display, but it might have been used in fights as well.
- Rival *Stygimoloch* probably did not butt each other with their heads but pushed against each other's sides instead.

Fact file

Found in: North America

Meaning of name: Demon of the river Styx

Length: 10 ft (3 m)

Weight: 170 lb (77 kg)

Lived: 67–65 million years ago

Diet: Plants

- *Stygimoloch* had small, triangular teeth for chewing tough leaves.
- As the dinosaur got older, its skull became rounder and grew more spikes.
- Evidence suggests that *Stygimoloch* lived in herds.

Psittacosaurus

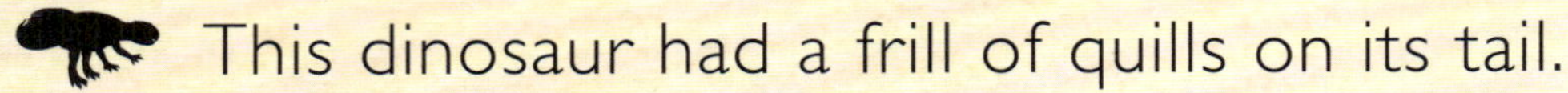

- This dinosaur had a frill of quills on its tail.
- It had a bony beak for chopping off the tops of shrubs.
- *Psittacosaurus* was a fast runner and could run on two legs while using its tail for balance.
- *Psittacosaurus* spent most of its time upright on its back legs and may have used its forelimbs to grasp objects.

Fact file

Found in: Asia
Meaning of name: Parrot lizard
Length: 6½ ft (2 m)
Weight: 110 lb (50 kg)
Lived: 120–100 million years ago
Diet: Plants

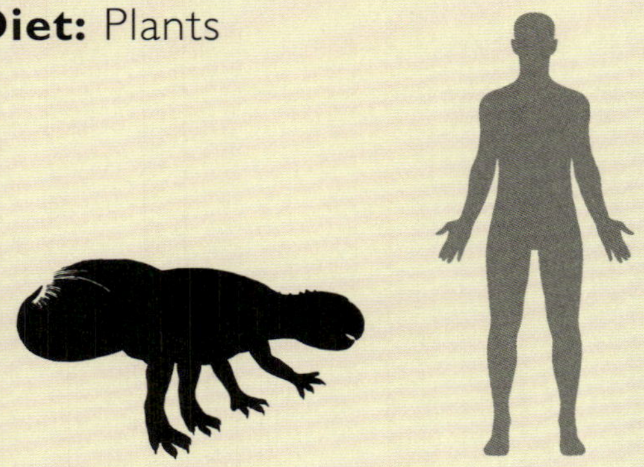

- *Psittacosaurus* had small, hornlike spikes around the back of its head.
- This dinosaur had large eyes, which would have allowed it to see well during the day and at night.
- Some scientists have suggested that *Psittacosaurus* could swim by using its frilly tail as a paddle.

Stegosaurus

- This dinosaur's brain was about the size of a small apple.
- *Stegosaurus* could use its spiked tail to defend itself from predators.
- The plates along *Stegosaurus*'s backbone may have offered some protection against attackers.
- Scientists believe the plates also absorbed sunlight and helped *Stegosaurus* control its body temperature.
- At first, scientists thought the plates stuck out sideways, making a "roof," which is how it got its name. (In Greek, *stegos* means "roof.")
- *Stegosaurus* could not chew its food and instead swallowed it in large chunks.
- *Stegosaurus* could not lift its head very high, so it grazed on small ferns that grew low to the ground.

Fact file

Found in: North America, Europe
Meaning of name: Roof lizard
Length: 30 ft (9 m)
Weight: Up to 6,800 lb (3,085 kg)
Lived: 155–145 million years ago
Diet: Plants

Ankylosaurus

- This dinosaur's back was protected by thick, bony plates and spikes.
- Some *Ankylosaurus* had a large bony club at the end of their tails.
- The tail club was used to hit attackers.
- *Ankylosaurus* was very wide and had short legs. This made it difficult to knock over in fights.
- *Ankylosaurus* lived in mountainous regions and ate all kinds of plants.

- A whack from the tail club was strong enough to break a *T. rex*'s leg!
- Even the eyelids of *Ankylosaurus* had small bony plates for extra protection.

Fact file

Found in: North America
Meaning of name: Fused lizard
Length: 20 ft (6 m)
Weight: 8,800 lb (4,000 kg)
Lived: 74–67 million years ago
Diet: Plants

Velociraptor

- *Velociraptor* is one of the most famous dinosaurs. It was much smaller than many people think, only about the size of a large turkey—although it was probably much fiercer.
- *Velociraptor* had long arms with hooked claws for reaching forward and grabbing prey.
- This hunter used its claws and teeth to attack prey.
- *Velociraptor* was covered with small feathers, which could have been used to attract a mate or keep its body warm.

- *Velociraptor* had a large brain relative to its body size, which suggests it was one of the more intelligent dinosaur species.
- *Velociraptor* could run at speeds up to 40 miles per hour (64 km/h) for short distances, so it could catch prey easily.

Fact file

Found in: Mongolia

Meaning of name: Swift seizer (aka, speedy thief)

Length: 6 ft (2 m)

Weight: 33 lb (15 kg)

Lived: 74–70 million years ago

Diet: Small mammals, birds, small dinosaurs

Brachiosaurus

- *Brachiosaurus* was twice as tall as a modern giraffe.
- This massive dinosaur stripped pine needles and leaves from the tops of tall trees.
- *Brachiosaurus* had large openings at the top of its head. They may have been used to make loud calls.
- *Brachiosaurus*'s neck usually pointed upward—it could lower its head to the ground, but this was rare.

- *Brachiosaurus*'s rear legs were more than six feet (2 m) long.
- It ate about 400 to 600 pounds (180 to 270 kg) of food every day.
- The dinosaur had just 12 large bones in its long neck.

Fact file

Found in: North America
Meaning of name: Arm lizard
Length: 66–72 ft (20–22 m)
Weight: 123,500 lb (56,020 kg)
Lived: 155–140 million years ago
Diet: Plants

Diplodocus

- *Diplodocus* was one of the longest land animals to ever live on Earth.
- The tail of a *Diplodocus* made up about half of this dinosaur's body length.
- Scientists believe that *Diplodocus* used its long, pointed tail as a whip to fight off attackers.
- *Diplodocus*'s spine and tail contained 95 bones, far more than any other dinosaur.
- Scientists believe that *Diplodocus* had air sacs deep inside its body that helped to pump air through its lungs.

* *Diplodocus*'s back legs were longer than its front ones, which shows it lowered its head to feed on plants close to the ground.

* *Diplodocus* could not chew its food. Instead, it swallowed stones to help grind up food in its stomach.

Fact file

Found in: North America

Meaning of name: Double beam

Length: 85 ft (26 m)

Weight: 44,000 lb (20,000 kg)

Lived: 155–145 million years ago

Diet: Plants

Dreadnoughtus

- *Dreadnoughtus* is thought to be one of the largest dinosaurs ever discovered.
- *Dreadnoughtus* weighed up to 143,000 pounds (64,860 kg) —that is about as much as 13 African elephants.
- A dinosaur this big had very few enemies.
- This giant creature is named after the unbeatable battleship called the HMS *Dreadnought*.

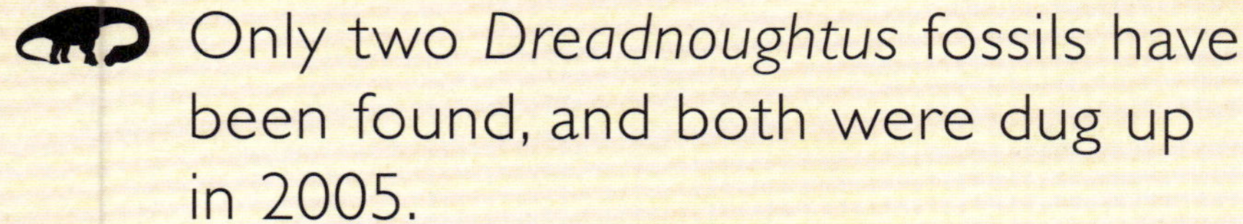

- Only two *Dreadnoughtus* fossils have been found, and both were dug up in 2005.

- Scientists wonder if the fossils of this giant dinosaur found so far are from young animals. If so, *Dreadnoughtus* may have been even larger than we know!

Fact file

Found in: South America
Meaning of name: Fear nothing
Length: 85 ft (26 m)
Weight: 143,000 lb (64,860 kg)
Lived: 84–66 million years ago
Diet: Plants

Oviraptor

- The first fossil of this dinosaur was found lying beside a nest full of eggs. Experts first thought that this dinosaur was raiding the nest and named the creature *Oviraptor*, or "egg thief." However, we now know she was a mother guarding her own eggs.
- *Oviraptor* probably had a brightly colored feathered tail that fanned out like a peacock's.
- *Oviraptor* had a bony crest on its head. This might have been used as a weapon, or it could have been another way of showing off.
- *Oviraptor* had large eyes for spotting danger—if it saw a hunter, it could run away quickly.
- This dinosaur was related to *Velociraptor* and other hunters, but it probably ate both plants and small animals.
- *Oviraptor* had no teeth, but it had bone spikes inside its mouth that may have been used for cracking open shellfish.

Fact file

Found in: Mongolia
Meaning of name: Egg thief
Length: 6½ ft (2 m)
Weight: 44 lb (20 kg)
Lived: 85–75 million years ago
Diet: Plants, lizards

Maiasaura

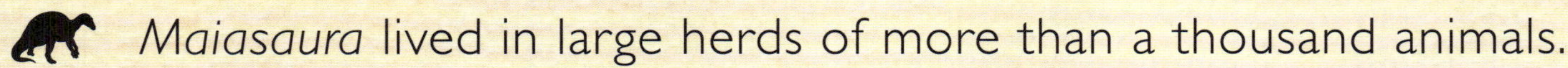

- *Maiasaura* lived in large herds of more than a thousand animals.
- The female *Maiasaura* laid their eggs at the same time, creating a huge nesting colony.
- Each female *Maiasaura* made a nest out of mud and leaves.
- The *Maiasaura* mother laid her eggs in a spiral or circle shape within the nest mound.

Fact file

Found in: North America
Meaning of name: Mother lizard
Length: 30 ft (9 m)
Weight: 5,500 lb (2,500 kg)
Lived: 80–75 million years ago
Diet: Plants

- After the eggs hatched, the babies stayed on the mound and were fed by their mother.
- *Maiasaura* could stand on their back legs to reach food in trees.
- Herds of *Maiasaura* probably returned to the same nesting sites each year.

Corythosaurus

 *Corythosaurus* was one of the hadrosaurid, or duck-billed, dinosaurs, which are named for their wide, flat mouths.

 This dinosaur had a bony crest on its head. Scientists think this might have become brightly colored during the breeding season.

 The duck-bill mouth was used to crush the needles, twigs, and cones that grew on pine trees.

 The crest was hollow and made *Corythosaurus*'s calls louder.

Fact file

Found in: North America
Meaning of name: Helmet lizard
Length: 33 ft (10 m)
Weight: 9,900 lb (4,490 kg)
Lived: 75–74 million years ago
Diet: Plants

- *Corythosaurus* lived in forests and waded through swamps.
- *Corythosaurus* likely had a more sensitive sense of hearing than most dinosaurs—even though its ears were hidden inside its skull.
- The large eyes of *Corythosaurus* tell us that this animal could see well during the day and at night.

Parasaurolophus

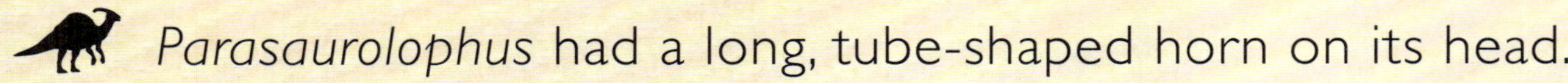

- *Parasaurolophus* had a long, tube-shaped horn on its head.
- The horn was hollow, with air passages running from the top of the dinosaur's head to its nostrils. The passages may have been used like a trumpet to produce a loud honking noise.
- *Parasaurolophus* walked on four legs but could run on its back legs to flee danger.

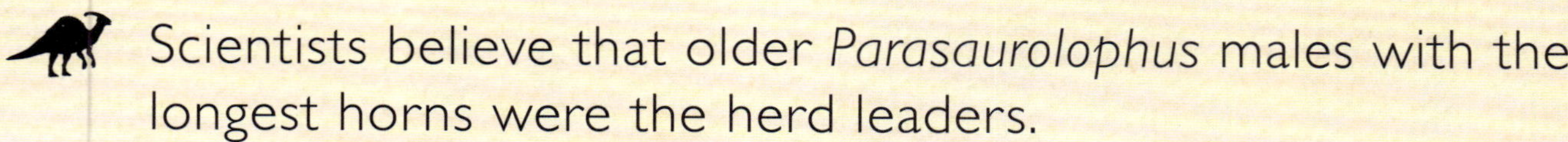

Scientists believe that older *Parasaurolophus* males with the longest horns were the herd leaders.

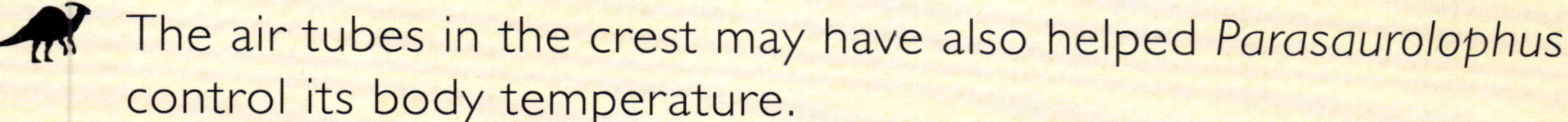

The air tubes in the crest may have also helped *Parasaurolophus* control its body temperature.

Fact file

Found in: North America

Meaning of name: Near crested lizard

Length: 36 ft (11 m)

Weight: 7,700 lb (3,490 kg)

Lived: 76–74 million years ago

Diet: Pine needles, leaves

Plateosaurus

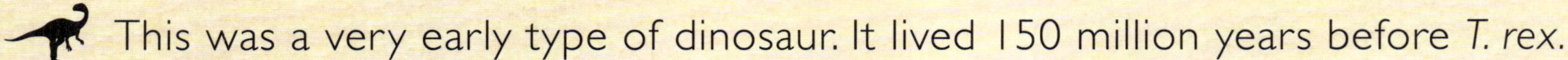

- This was a very early type of dinosaur. It lived 150 million years before *T. rex*.
- *Plateosaurus* was an early relative of the giant plant-eating dinosaurs, like *Diplodocus* and *Brachiosaurus*.
- *Plateosaurus* walked on two legs and used its clawed hands to pull branches to its mouth.
- Its thick tail worked like a third leg to keep it balanced as it reached up into tall trees.

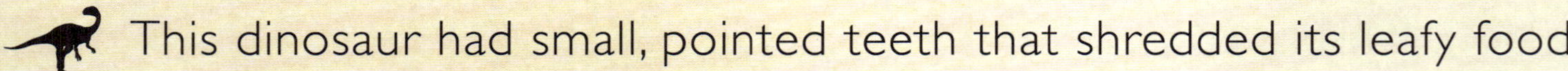

- This dinosaur had small, pointed teeth that shredded its leafy food.
- *Plateosaurus* had a big hooked claw on its thumb, which might have been used in fights.

Fact file

Found in: Europe

Meaning of name: Broad lizard

Length: 23 ft (7 m)

Weight: 8,800 lb (4,000 kg)

Lived: 210 million years ago

Diet: Plants

Therizinosaurus

- This dinosaur is named for the giant claws on its hands, which look like curved knives, or scythes. (In Greek, *therizo* means "to cut or mow.")
- *Therizinosaurus* had three claws on each hand, which could grow to be more than three feet (1 m) long.
- Evidence suggests that this dinosaur was probably covered in feathers like its relatives *Velociraptor* and *Deinonychus*.
- *Therizinosaurus* likely had flat teeth and a beak, suggesting that it was not a hunter; it would have eaten plants and perhaps insects.

- Scientists believe that *Therizinosaurus*'s claws were probably used to reach leafy branches.
- *Therizinosaurus* may also have used its claws for digging up roots or termite mounds.
- *Therizinosaurus* was very tall and could fight off most enemies with its slashing claws.

Fact file

Found in: Mongolia
Meaning of name: Scythe lizard
Length: Up to 33 ft (10 m)
Weight: 11,000 lb (5,000 kg)
Lived: 85–70 million years ago
Diet: Plants, insects

Coelophysis

- A slender hunter, *Coelophysis* was one of the first dinosaurs to evolve.
- This fast-running dinosaur preyed on small animals.
- Large herds of *Coelophysis* gathered at watering holes to drink or eat fish.
- This dinosaur was named for its hollow leg bones. (In Greek, *coelos* means "hollow," and *physis* means "form.") Today, though, we know that most dinosaur leg bones were hollow.

- More than 1,000 *Coelophysis* fossils were found in one location in New Mexico.

- *Coelophysis* was not a strong dinosaur, but it probably hunted in packs to take down larger prey.

Fact file

Found in: North America, Africa

Meaning of name: Hollow form

Length: 10 ft (3 m)

Weight: 60 lb (27 kg)

Lived: 225–190 million years ago

Diet: Fish, small reptiles

Microraptor

- This small feathered dinosaur had four wings—two at the front and two at the back.
- *Microraptor* had claws on its wings, which it used for climbing trees.
- This dinosaur used its four wings to glide between trees to escape danger.
- *Microraptor* could have used its gliding wings to pounce on lizards living in trees.

- This dinosaur probably also scooped up fish while gliding over water.
- *Microraptor* was likely a nighttime hunter; fossils suggest that its eyes provided excellent vision in the dark.
- Scientists believe that *Microraptor* could not take off from the ground.
- *Microraptor* is the smallest known dinosaur species.

Fact file

Found in: China
Meaning of name: Tiny seizer
Length: 2 ft (60 cm)
Weight: 2 lb (910 g)
Lived: 125–122 million years ago
Diet: Insects

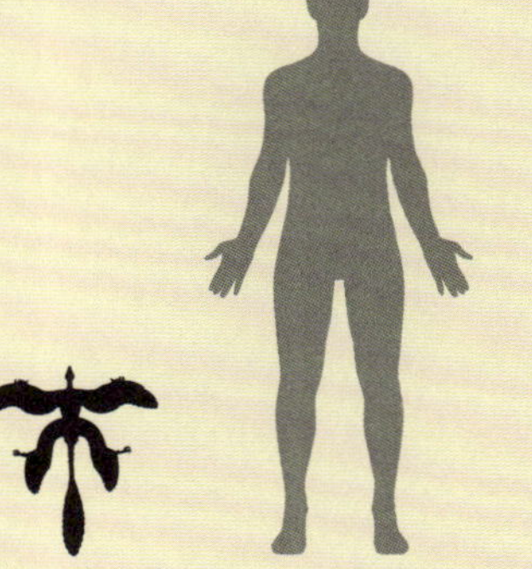

Compsognathus

- This dinosaur was about the size of a large turkey.
- Scientists believe that *Compsognathus* chased its lizard prey through the undergrowth.
- *Compsognathus* hunted by sight using its large eyes and could move quickly to capture prey.
- No other dinosaur fossils have been found near *Compsognathus* fossils, which suggests that it was the top predator in its habitat.
- *Compsognathus* lived on islands in a sea that once covered eastern Europe and the Middle East.

Complete remains of lizards have been found inside *Compsognathus* fossils, which means that this dinosaur swallowed its prey whole.

Fact file

Found in: Southeastern Europe
Meaning of name: Elegant jaw
Length: 2 ft (60 cm)
Weight: 7 lb (3 kg)
Lived: 145–140 million years ago
Diet: Insects, lizards

Avimimus

- This dinosaur lived in what is now Mongolia, around 75 million years ago.
- Most of the bones in *Avimimus*'s small arms were fused together like in a bird's wing.
- *Avimimus* could not fly, but it probably used its feathers to keep warm, or for display.
- *Avimimus* had a beak with small teeth, which meant it could eat both plants and animals.

Fact file

Found in: Asia
Meaning of name: Bird mimic
Length: 5 ft (1.5 m)
Weight: 33 lb (15 kg)
Lived: 80–75 million years ago
Diet: Plants, insects, small lizards

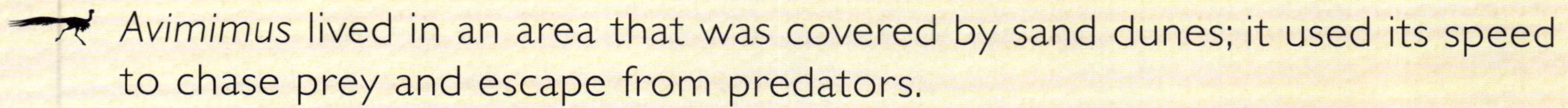

- *Avimimus* lived in an area that was covered by sand dunes; it used its speed to chase prey and escape from predators.

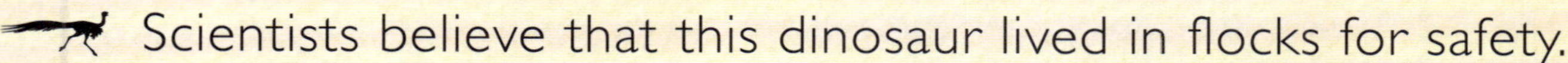

- Scientists believe that this dinosaur lived in flocks for safety.

Archaeopteryx

- Many scientists think that *Archaeopteryx* was not a dinosaur but one of the first birds.
- *Archaeopteryx* had a long, bony tail, and sharp teeth.
- Scientists don't know if *Archaeopteryx* could fly from the ground—it probably glided out of trees instead.
- *Archaeopteryx* did not have big flying muscles like today's birds, so it could not stay in the air for long.

Fact file

Found in: Europe

Meaning of name: Ancient feather

Length: 1½ ft (46 cm)

Weight: 1 lb (450 kg)

Lived: 151–149 million years ago

Diet: Insects, lizards

- This animal's small eyes suggest that it hunted during the day.
- Scientists think that *Archaeopteryx* used its wings to help it stay up while it ran over the surface of a lake to hunt fish.
- Evidence suggests *Archaeopteryx* would have grabbed prey with its mouth and held it there with its claws.

Quetzalcoatlus

- *Quetzalcoatlus* was one of the largest flying animals to have ever lived.
- Its wingspan was about the size of a small airplane.
- *Quetzalcoatlus* was not a dinosaur. It was an ancient flying reptile called a pterosaur.
- Scientists believe that this giant flier most likely fed on prey on the ground, like a stork or crane.
- *Quetzalcoatlus* could walk on all fours with its wings folded out of the way.
- *Quetzalcoatlus* could glide through the air for long periods at a time looking for food.
- This creature is named after *Quetzalcoatl*, a feathered god worshipped by the Aztecs, who lived in what is now Mexico.

Fact file

Found in: North America

Meaning of name: Bird goddess reptile

Length: 30 ft (9 m) (wingspan)

Weight: 550 lb (250 kg)

Lived: 70–68 million years ago

Diet: Small dinosaurs, lizards, mammals

Pterodactylus

- *Pterodactylus* was a flying reptile with wings made of large flaps of skin, like those of a bat.
- Scientists think that it fed by swooping down to grab fish from the water.
- This creature was discovered in 1784, before dinosaurs were identified. It was the first flying reptile ever known.
- The front of its wings were made from extremely long, thin finger bones.
- *Pterodactylus*, like other prehistoric flying reptiles, was not a dinosaur. These creatures belonged to a group of reptiles known as pterosaurs.

This reptile ate small fish, and it may have been able to land on water.

Pterodactylus may have had a fine, furlike coat with a texture similar to leather.

Fact file

Found in: Europe

Meaning of name: Wing finger

Length: 3½ ft (1 m) (wingspan)

Weight: 6 lb (3 kg)

Lived: 151–148 million years ago

Diet: Insects, fish

Elasmosaurus

- *Elasmosaurus* belonged to a group of marine reptiles called plesiosaurs.
- It had a long, flexible neck that contained 71 bones.
- Its tail was much shorter—that had just 18 bones.
- *Elasmosaurus* lived in shallow seas and preyed on fish and squid.
- Evidence suggests that *Elasmosaurus* attacked fish from below, lunging upward with its long neck to catch them.
- This sea creature had flippers instead of legs and could not walk on land.
- Scientists believe that *Elasmosaurus* did not lay eggs but gave birth to live babies in the water, like other plesiosaurs living at the same time.

Fact file

Found in: Shallow seas, especially in North America

Meaning of name: Thin plate lizard

Length: 45 ft (14 m)

Weight: 6,000 lb (2,720 kg)

Lived: 80–65 million years ago

Diet: Fish, squid, shellfish

Kronosaurus

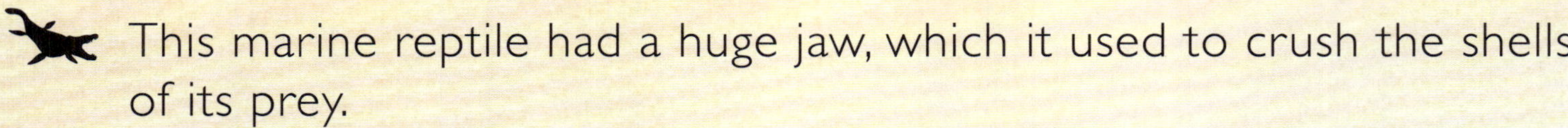

- This marine reptile had a huge jaw, which it used to crush the shells of its prey.
- It is a pliosaur, which were the largest and toughest hunters in the ancient seas.
- *Kronosaurus* had cone-shaped teeth.
- The teeth at the front of this creature's jaw were massive and fanglike, but the teeth at the back were smaller and could crush bones.

The reptile swam using four powerful flippers. It may also have been able to use its flippers to walk on land, like seals do today.

Kronosaurus probably fed like some modern crocodiles do, by twisting off large chunks of meat from its prey.

Fact file

Found in: Shallow seas, worldwide

Meaning of name: Kronos's lizard

Length: 30 ft (9 m)

Weight: 13,700 lb (6,215 kg)

Lived: 120–100 million years ago

Diet: Fish, squid, and reptiles

Mixosaurus

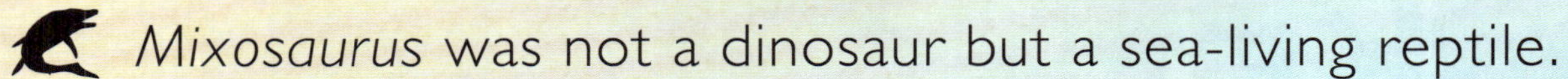
Mixosaurus was not a dinosaur but a sea-living reptile.

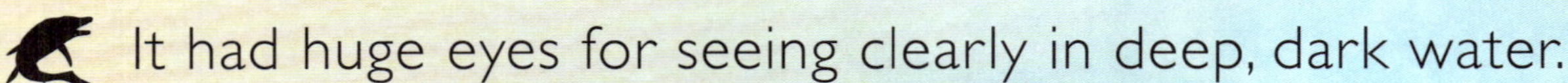
It had huge eyes for seeing clearly in deep, dark water.

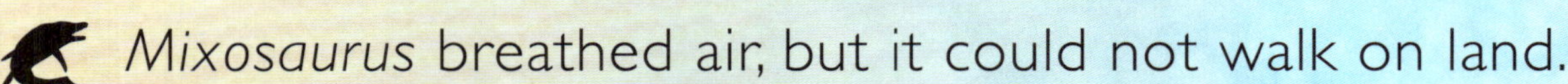
Mixosaurus breathed air, but it could not walk on land.

This reptile gave birth to live babies in warm, shallow water.

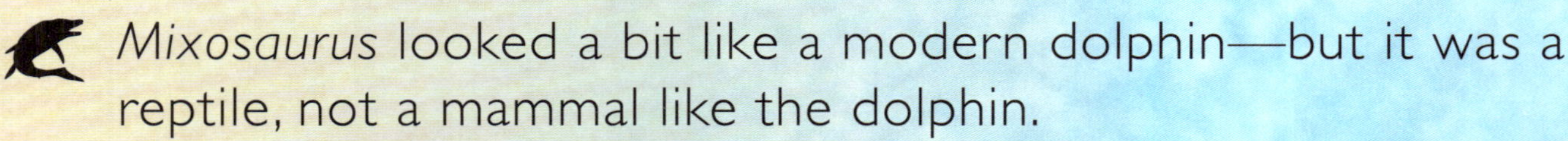
Mixosaurus looked a bit like a modern dolphin—but it was a reptile, not a mammal like the dolphin.

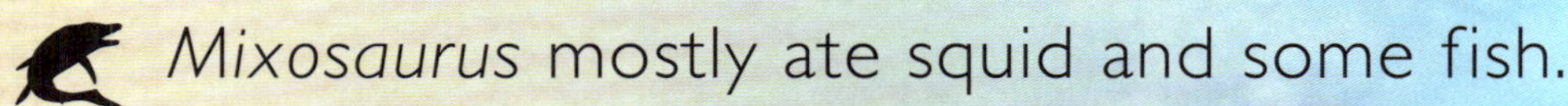
Mixosaurus mostly ate squid and some fish.

Fact file

Found in: Europe, Asia

Meaning of name: Mixed reptile

Length: 3 ft (90 cm)

Weight: 200 lb (90 kg)

Lived: 247–237 million years ago

Diet: Fish, squid

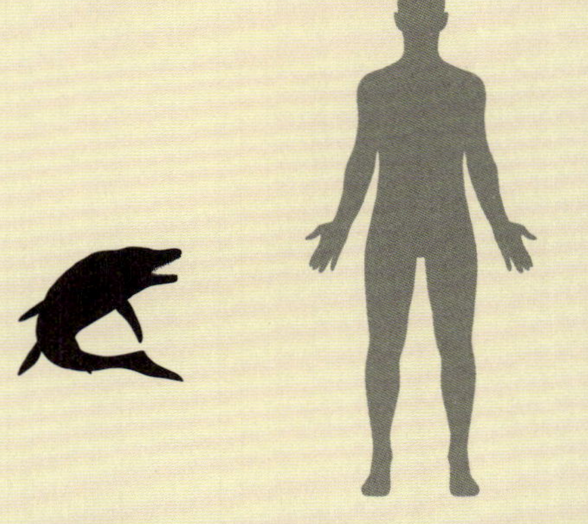

Tylosaurus

- This is one of the largest marine reptiles ever found.
- It is more closely related to today's monitor lizards than to dinosaurs or other ancient reptiles.
- Evidence suggests that this massive hunter may have attacked prey by ramming into it at full speed.
- *Tylosaurus* used its flippers for steering but was powered through the water by its long, flat tail.
- *Tylosaurus* had a strong bite and gripped prey with its teeth so it could not get away.
- This hunter did not chew its food; it either swallowed prey whole or bit off large chunks.
- *Tylosaurus* swam in shallow water and attacked all kinds of animals—it even pulled land animals into the water.

Fact file

Found in: Seas of North America
Meaning of name: Knob lizard
Length: 45 ft (14 m)
Weight: 20,000 lb (9,070 kg)
Lived: 85–80 million years ago
Diet: Fish, turtles, other reptiles

Dimetrodon

- *Dimetrodon* was a giant hunter that lived long before the dinosaurs.
- It was more closely related to today's mammals than to dinosaurs or other ancient reptiles.
- *Dimetrodon* had a huge "sail" made of skin and bone spines on its back.
- Scientists believe that the sail helped *Dimetrodon* warm up in the sun so that it could run faster than its cold-blooded prey.

To cool down, *Dimetrodon* probably turned its back away from the sun so that its sail gave off heat instead of taking it in.

Dimetrodon had two kinds of teeth: long ones for killing its prey and shorter ones for crushing them up.

Unlike a dinosaur, *Dimetrodon*'s legs stuck out sideways from its body.

Fact file

Found in: North America, Europe

Meaning of name: Two measures (sizes) of teeth

Length: 15 ft (4.5 m)

Weight: 550 lb (250 kg)

Lived: 295–272 million years ago

Diet: Fish, amphibians, small reptiles

Gastonia

- This armored dinosaur lived in dry forests and chewed on twigs and leaves.
- Its body and tail were covered in spikes and armor plates.
- Sideways-pointing spikes, especially on its tail, were used to fight off predators.
- The upward-pointing spikes on its back may have helped males look bigger in battles over mates.

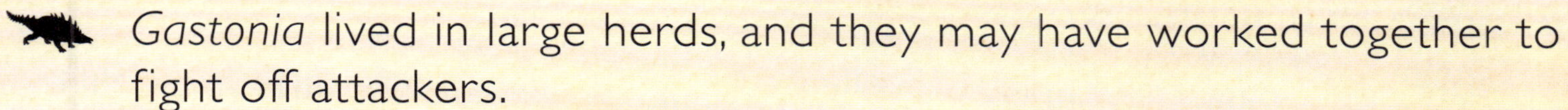

- *Gastonia* lived in large herds, and they may have worked together to fight off attackers.
- Evidence suggests that *Gastonia* males head-butted each other in tests of strength.
- This dinosaur had no armor on its belly, but it was very hard for predators to push it over and bite it.

Fact file

Found in: North America

Meaning of name: Gaston's reptile

Length: 15 ft (4.5 m)

Weight: 4,000 lb (1,815 kg)

Lived: 147–127 million years ago

Diet: Plants

Sarcosuchus

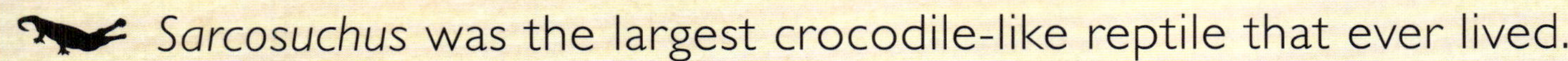

- *Sarcosuchus* was the largest crocodile-like reptile that ever lived.
- These creatures were not dinosaurs, but they lived at the same time and were closely related to them.
- *Sarcosuchus* was twice as big as the largest modern crocodiles.
- *Sarcosuchus* had a round lump on its snout. Scientists believe this was probably used to make calls in the water.

Fact file

Found in: Africa, South America
Meaning of name: Flesh crocodile
Length: 39 ft (12 m)
Weight: 17,600 lb (7,980 kg)
Lived: 112 million years ago
Diet: Dinosaurs, large fish

- This giant crocodile ambushed dinosaurs that came to drink at the water's edge.
- The bite of *Sarcosuchus* was probably twice as powerful as that of a *T. rex*.
- Their eyes looked upward and not forward, so they could watch for prey while hiding under the water.

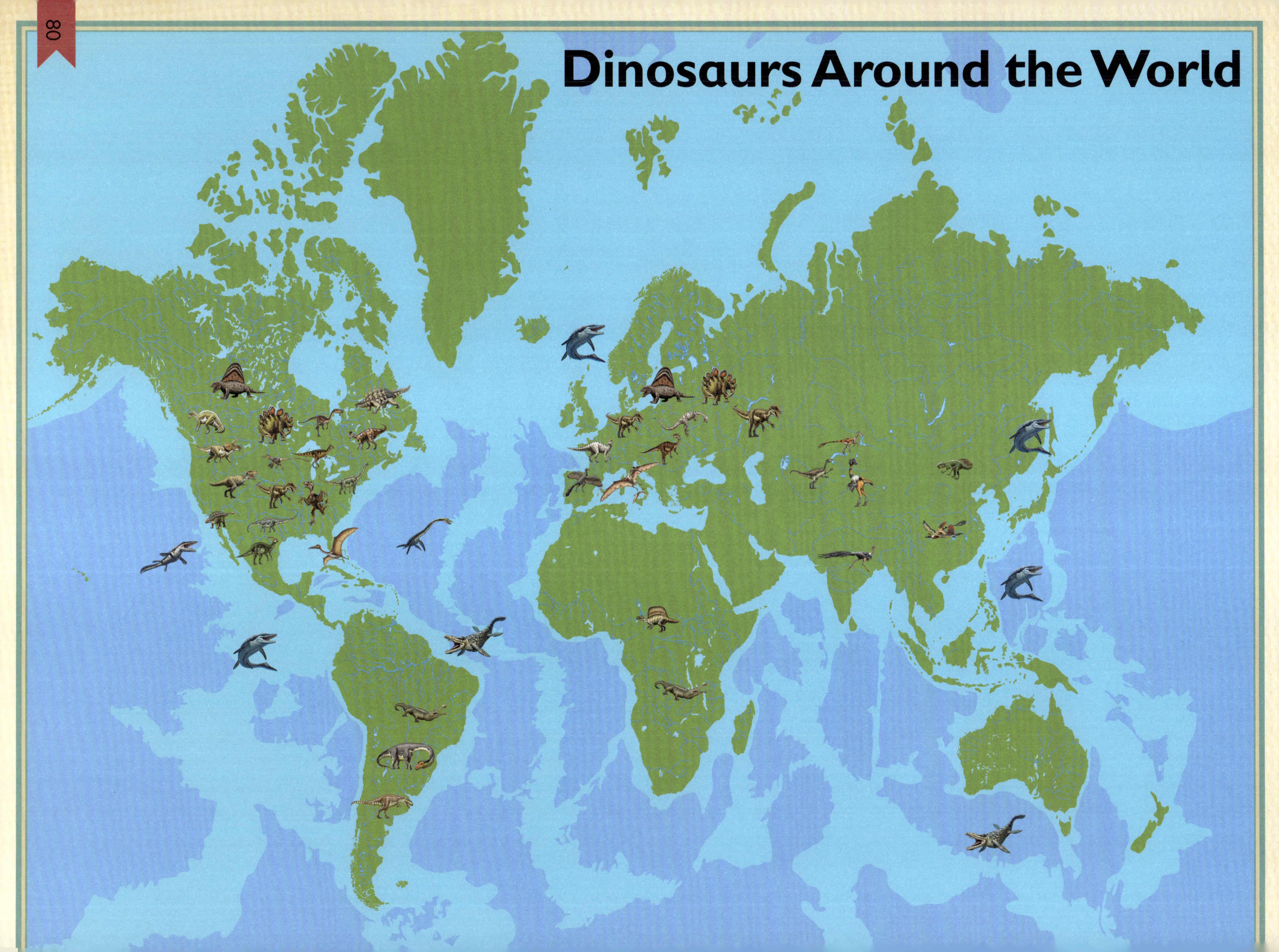
Dinosaurs Around the World